Goat stood on the top of a cliff and looked out to sea. "What shall I do today ?" he said to himself. He was very lonely.

A large bird flew down and landed on one of his horns. "Hello Goat, I hope you are well," she said. "What do you want?" said Goat.

"Could you spare me a few of your hairs to put into my nest ?" asked the bird. She put a few hairs in her beak and pulled.

The seagulls who were watching laughed as Goat jumped up in the air. "Go away," he said. But the bird only flew down on to his back. "Give me some hair," she said, "and I will tell you a story."

Although Goat's hair was dirty and tangled he didn't want to lose it, but he did like stories.   While he was making up his mind a fishing boat went by and the seagulls flew off for a free ride.

"I haven't been told a story since I was a kid," Goat said. So the bird began. "Once there was a smelly old goat who never washed. He just wandered about all day doing nothing."

The bird pulled some more hairs out and flew away. Goat ran after her and shouted, "What about my story ?" But the bird didn't hear him. Goat ate some nettles and berries, then wandered down to the sea

He was paddling in a rock pool when the bird came back. She went on with her story, "No one talked to the smelly old goat so he was very lonely."

The bird quickly pulled out some more hairs and flew away again. It hurt goat so much that tears ran down his cheeks and made his beard wet.

Goat climbed up the path past the lighthouse through the thistles to the top of the cliff. The bird was waiting for him.
"You can't pull out any more of my hair, it hurts too much," grumbled Goat.

"I don't need any more, I've finished my nest." "What about my story ?" asked Goat. The bird flew on to a rock on the cliff edge and not too near Goat. "You're the goat in my story," laughed the bird.

"I'm not old and I'm not smelly either," cried Goat. He put his head down and started to run towards the bird. But she flew away. Goat tripped over a rock and fell into the sea.

Goat frightened all the fish as he splashed in the sea. He struggled out of the water, cold and covered with shells and seaweed. A crab was on his tail.

Goat stood on the top of the cliff and dried himself in the warm sun. The bird called out, "Sorry Goat, but you look much better now you are clean."

The bird flew up to the tree into her new nest. "This is the most comfortable nest I have ever made," she said.

The other goats gathered round Goat. "We are going along the cliff to find a new home, please come with us." Goat was very proud as he led the way and all the other goats followed him.